Francis Frith's
AROUND NEWQUAY

PHOTOGRAPHIC MEMORIES

Francis Frith's
AROUND NEWQUAY

◆

Martin Dunning

FRITH
BOOK CO

First published in the United Kingdom in 2000 by
Frith Book Company Ltd

British Library Cataloguing in Publication Data

Around Newquay
Martin Dunning
ISBN 1-85937-140-x

Frith Book Company Ltd
Frith's Barn, Teffont,
Salisbury, Wiltshire SP3 5QP
Tel: +44 (0) 1722 716 376
Email: info@frithbook.co.uk
www.frithbook.co.uk

Printed and bound in Great Britain

Front Cover: Newquay, Bank Street 1931 84395

CONTENTS

FRANCIS FRITH: *Victorian Pioneer*

FRANCIS FRITH, Victorian founder of the world-famous photographic archive, was a complex and multitudinous man. A devout Quaker and a highly successful Victorian businessman, he was both philosophic by nature and pioneering in outlook.

By 1855 Francis Frith had already established a wholesale grocery business in Liverpool, and sold it for the astonishing sum of £200,000, which is the equivalent today of over £15,000,000. Now a multi-millionaire, he was able to indulge his passion for travel. As a child he had pored over travel books written by early explorers, and his fancy and imagination had been stirred by family holidays to the sublime mountain regions of Wales and Scotland. 'What a land of spirit-stirring and enriching scenes and places!' he had written. He was to return to these scenes of grandeur in later years to 'recapture the thousands of vivid and tender memories', but with a different purpose. Now in his thirties, and captivated by the new science of photography, Frith set out on a series of pioneering journeys to the Nile regions that occupied him from 1856 until 1860.

INTRIGUE AND ADVENTURE

He took with him on his travels a specially-designed wicker carriage that acted as both dark-room and sleeping chamber. These far-flung journeys were packed with intrigue and adventure. In his life story, written when he was sixty-three, Frith tells of being held captive by bandits, and of fighting 'an awful midnight battle to the very point of surrender with a deadly pack of hungry, wild dogs'. Sporting flowing Arab costume, Frith arrived at Akaba by camel seventy years before Lawrence, where he encountered 'desert princes and rival sheikhs, blazing with jewel-hilted swords'.

During these extraordinary adventures he was assiduously exploring the desert regions bordering the Nile and patiently recording the antiquities and peoples with his camera. He was the first photographer to venture beyond the sixth cataract. Africa was still the mysterious 'Dark Continent', and Stanley and Livingstone's historic meeting was a decade into the future. The conditions for picture taking confound belief. He laboured for hours in his wicker dark-room in the sweltering heat of the desert, while the volatile chemicals fizzed dangerously in their trays. Often he was forced to work in remote tombs and caves where conditions were cooler. Back in London he exhibited his photographs and was 'rapturously cheered' by members of the Royal Society. His reputation as a photographer was made overnight. An eminent modern historian has likened their impact on the population of the time to that on our own generation of the first photographs taken on the surface of the moon.

VENTURE OF A LIFE-TIME

Characteristically, Frith quickly spotted the opportunity to create a new business as a specialist publisher of photographs. He lived in an era of immense and sometimes violent change. For the poor in the early part of Victoria's reign work was a drudge and the hours long, and people had precious little free time to enjoy themselves.

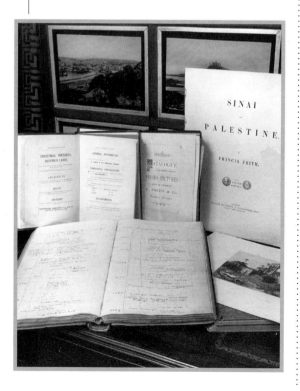

Most had no transport other than a cart or gig at their disposal, and had not travelled far beyond the boundaries of their own town or village. However, by the 1870s, the railways had threaded their way across the country, and Bank Holidays and half-day Saturdays had been made obligatory by Act of Parliament. All of a sudden the ordinary working man and his family were able to enjoy days out and see a little more of the world.

With characteristic business acumen, Francis Frith foresaw that these new tourists would enjoy having souvenirs to commemorate their days out. In 1860 he married Mary Ann Rosling and set out with the intention of photographing every city, town and village in Britain. For the next thirty years he travelled the country by train and by pony and trap, producing fine photographs of seaside resorts and beauty spots that were keenly bought by millions of Victorians. These prints were painstakingly pasted into family albums and pored over during the dark nights of winter, rekindling precious memories of summer excursions.

THE RISE OF FRITH & CO

Frith's studio was soon supplying retail shops all over the country. To meet the demand he gathered about him a small team of photographers, and published the work of independent artist-photographers of the calibre of Roger Fenton and Francis Bedford. In order to gain some understanding of the scale of Frith's business one only has to look at the catalogue issued by Frith & Co in 1886: it runs to some 670 pages, listing not only many thousands of views of the British Isles but also many photographs of most European countries, and China, Japan, the USA and Canada – note the sample page shown above from the hand-written *Frith & Co* ledgers detailing pictures taken. By 1890 Frith had created the greatest specialist photographic publishing company in the world, with over 2,000 outlets – more than the combined number that Boots and WH Smith have today! The picture on the right shows the *Frith & Co* display board at Ingleton in the Yorkshire Dales. Beautifully constructed with mahogany frame and gilt inserts, it could display up to a dozen local scenes.

POSTCARD BONANZA

The ever-popular holiday postcard we know today took many years to develop. In 1870 the Post Office issued the first plain cards, with a pre-printed stamp on one face. In 1894 they allowed other publishers' cards to be sent through the mail with an attached adhesive halfpenny stamp. Demand grew rapidly, and in 1895 a new size of postcard was permitted called the court card, but there was little room for illustration. In 1899, a year after Frith's death, a new card measuring 5.5 x 3.5 inches became the standard format, but it was not until 1902 that the divided back came into being, with address and message on one face and a full-size illustration on the other. *Frith & Co* were in the vanguard of postcard development, and Frith's sons Eustace and Cyril continued their father's monumental task, expanding the number of views offered to the public and recording more and more places in Britain, as the coasts and countryside were opened up to mass travel.

Francis Frith died in 1898 at his villa in Cannes, his great project still growing. The archive he created continued in business for another seventy years. By 1970 it contained over a third of a million pictures of 7,000 cities, towns and villages. The massive photographic record Frith has left to us stands as a living monument to a special and very remarkable man.

Frith's Archive: *A Unique Legacy*

FRANCIS FRITH'S legacy to us today is of immense significance and value, for the magnificent archive of evocative photographs he created provides a unique record of change in 7,000 cities, towns and villages throughout Britain over a century and more. Frith and his fellow studio photographers revisited locations many times down the years to update their views, compiling for us an enthralling and colourful pageant of British life and character.

We tend to think of Frith's sepia views of Britain as nostalgic, for most of us use them to conjure up memories of places in our own lives with which we have family associations. It often makes us forget that to Francis Frith they were records of daily life as it was actually being lived in the cities, towns and villages of his day. The Victorian age was one of great and often bewildering change for ordinary people, and though the pictures evoke an impression of slower times, life was as busy and hectic as it is today.

We are fortunate that Frith was a photographer of the people, dedicated to recording the minutiae of everyday life. For it is this sheer wealth of visual data, the painstaking chronicle of changes in dress, transport, street layouts, buildings, housing, engineering and landscape that captivates us so much today. His remarkable images offer us a powerful link with the past and with the lives of our ancestors.

TODAY'S TECHNOLOGY

Computers have now made it possible for Frith's many thousands of images to be accessed almost instantly. In the Frith archive today, each photograph is carefully 'digitised' then stored on a CD Rom. Frith archivists can locate a single photograph amongst thousands within seconds. Views can be catalogued and sorted under a variety of categories of place and content to the immediate benefit of researchers. Inexpensive reference prints can be created for them at the touch of a mouse button, and a wide range of books and other printed materials assembled and published for a wider, more general readership - in the next twelve months over a hundred Frith local history titles will be published! The

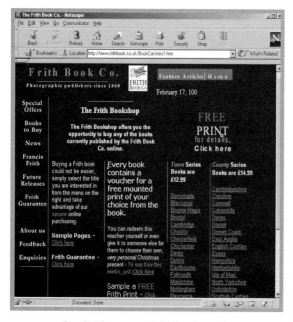

See Frith at www. frithbook.co.uk

day-to-day workings of the archive are very different from how they were in Francis Frith's time: imagine the herculean task of sorting through eleven tons of glass negatives as Frith had to do to locate a particular sequence of pictures! Yet the archive still prides itself on maintaining the same high standards of excellence laid down by Francis Frith, including the painstaking cataloguing and indexing of every view.

It is curious to reflect on how the internet now allows researchers in America and elsewhere greater instant access to the archive than Frith himself ever enjoyed. Many thousands of individual views can be called up on screen within seconds on one of the Frith internet sites, enabling people living continents away to revisit the streets of their ancestral home town, or view places in Britain where they have enjoyed holidays. Many overseas researchers welcome the chance to view special theme selections, such as transport, sports, costume and ancient monuments.

We are certain that Francis Frith would have heartily approved of these modern developments, for he himself was always working at the very limits of Victorian photographic technology.

THE VALUE OF THE ARCHIVE TODAY

Because of the benefits brought by the computer, Frith's images are increasingly studied by social historians, by researchers into genealogy and ancestory, by architects, town planners, and by teachers and schoolchildren involved in local history projects. In addition, the archive offers every one of us a unique opportunity to examine the places where we and our families have lived and worked down the years. Immensely successful in Frith's own era, the archive is now, a century and more on, entering a new phase of popularity.

THE PAST IN TUNE WITH THE FUTURE

Historians consider the Francis Frith Collection to be of prime national importance. It is the only archive of its kind remaining in private ownership and has been valued at a million pounds. However, this figure is now rapidly increasing as digital technology enables more and more people around the world to enjoy its benefits.

Francis Frith's archive is now housed in an historic timber barn in the beautiful village of Teffont in Wiltshire. Its founder would not recognize the archive office as it is today. In place of the many thousands of dusty boxes containing glass plate negatives and an all-pervading odour of photographic chemicals, there are now ranks of computer screens. He would be amazed to watch his images travelling round the world at unimaginable speeds through network and internet lines.

The archive's future is both bright and exciting. Francis Frith, with his unshakeable belief in making photographs available to the greatest number of people, would undoubtedly approve of what is being done today with his lifetime's work. His photographs, depicting our shared past, are now bringing pleasure and enlightenment to millions around the world a century and more after his death.

NEWQUAY – *An Introduction*

THE NORTH COAST of Cornwall is a wild and beautiful place. Vast precipices of slate and sandstone, inhabited only by seabirds and the odd wheeling peregrine or raven, alternate with beaches of golden sand, and in the valleys and the lee of headlands lie communities sheltering from the Atlantic westerlies. The whole coast, from Bude in the north to Land's End in the far west, is at the mercy of these westerlies and the huge oceanic swells they bring with them. The only really sheltered anchorage is in the mouth of the Camel estuary, and to anchor here means having to negotiate the fearsome Doom Bar. Inland the country, though hilly, is rich and fertile, and there is a living to be made. Making a living from the sea on this inhospitable coastline is, however, another matter.

The Newquay area was first settled, as were many other Cornish communities, in the Bronze Age. A Bronze Age barrow or burial mound, perhaps 4,000 years old, can still be seen at Barrowfields just off Narrowcliff. In about 200BC the Iron Age came to Newquay in the shape of the cliff castle at Trevelgue Head; with it came the Celts, who were the ancestors of generations of Cornish men and women and whose language, though rarely spoken, still survives in Cornish place names. Indeed, Newquay's original name is in that very Celtic tongue: Tewynplustri, from the Cornish 'towan' for sandhill and 'lystry' for boats, translating as boat cove in the sandhills. Another version is Porth Lystry, meaning boat beach. Whatever the exact origin of the name, the implication is clear - with no sheltered anchorage, boats had to be beached to stay clear of the weather. The sheltered but narrow and shallow Gannel to the south and the little inlet of Porth to the north were the main ports in mediaeval times, but they were at the mercy of heavy weather.

A big step forward came in 1439, when Bishop Lacey of Exeter granted an indulgence for the building of 'a new keye for the rode of shipping'. The New Quay was built under the cliffs safe from the westerlies: the town has been known by that name ever since. Not that it was a town for many years; until the 19th century it was still essentially a fishing village, living on the great shoals of pilchards which were for many centuries the Cornishman's staple food. Huers at lookouts such as the Huer's Hut made a 'hue and cry' on huge brass horns when a shoal was sighted, and used a complex system of flag signals to direct the seine boats (of which there were up to 40 working from Newquay) in the tricky task of ringing the shoal. Catches of pilchards could be enormous; there is a recorded catch in one month of 8,000 hogsheads landed at Newquay, some 24 million fish. Lead and iron were brought from the mines inland, and coal and other cargoes landed on the beach at Porth and at Towan Beach, but the pilchard was king.

Things changed in the 1840s when the harbour was bought by the miner and magnate Joseph Thomas Treffry, also known as the 'King of Mid-Cornwall'. Treffry, whose mining interests lay nearer the south coast, was worried by shipping losses on the treacherous passage around Land's End. He enlarged the harbour and established a rail link via a tunnel in the cliffs direct to the harbour. Copper ores from his Fowey Great Consols mine crossed the peninsula on a tramway to Newquay, where they were either lowered down the steep incline of the tunnel in wagons or discharged down chutes ready for loading onto ships which would take them to the smelters in South Wales. China clay was also moved in this way; in 1872 Treffry built Island Pier, joined to the harbourside by a timber trestlework jetty, so that more ships could take on cargo.

In 1874 the old Trenance Viaduct, a precarious timber bridge to the south of the town, was replaced by a more substantial stone and iron girder structure, and the rail-

TRENANCE VIADUCT 1907 59338

way arrived in 1875. As with so many Cornish towns - Falmouth is one example, and Penzance another - the arrival of the iron horse was to change Newquay's fortunes forever - and not a moment too soon, for in 1870 the pilchard stocks had collapsed and life was

the hotels were sprouting like mushrooms. The first of the big hotels was the Great Western on Cliff Road, and in 1898 the construction of the imposing Headland Hotel was begun at a magnificent site on Towan Head. Truro architect and businessman Sylvanus

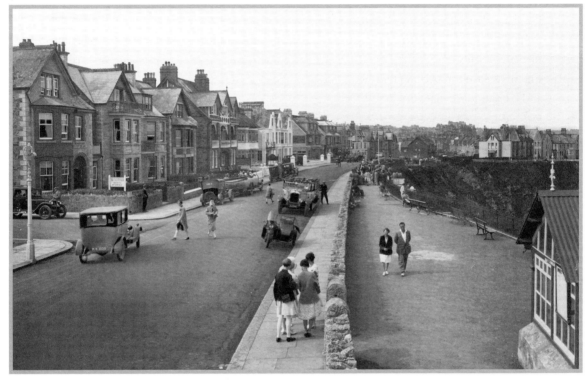

NARROWCLIFF 1928 81262

hard.

In Victorian Britain, seaside holidays were becoming popular. The middle classes had more money and perhaps one week's holiday a year, and for the first time there was access to mass transport in the form of the railways. The journey to London, which previously might have taken up to a week, could now be accomplished in a day, and local entrepreneurs were quick to spot the opportunity.

In 1851 there were but two hostelries in the little village - the Red Lion (then known as Prout's Hotel) and the Old Inn - but by 1901

Trevail was responsible for the design, and the grandeur of the building reflects his style - pavilion roofs, Italianate masks in terra cotta, an Imperial staircase with a cast iron balustrade and Ionic columns in Devon Marble - all a far cry from the functional stone buildings around the harbour. What had been essentially a fishing village and harbour was becoming a major resort: by 1901 the population numbered over 3,000. Narrowcliff was developed as a residential area with fine private villas, but the hoteliers were not slow to recognise the potential of the fine views from the clifftop, and the villas quickly became hotels. A cinema was built, and theatres such as the Big Six and the Cosy Nook appeared. Visitors came not only to stay for a week or two, but also on day trips on bank holidays and for occasions such as Lifeboat Day.

Newquay became a favourite with the Royal family - King George V stayed in the Royal Suite at the Headland, and in the twenties and thirties the young princes, two of whom were later to become King, were guests at the Chief Constable's house above the harbour. Prince Edward was a particularly frequent visitor, and often played golf on the town course.

World War Two brought a new set of visitors in the shape of servicemen. Some came to stay at the Headland, but not to admire the view, for the hotel had become an amputation hospital. The Watergate Bay Hotel was requisitioned as an Officers' Mess by the RAF to house personnel from the airfield at St Mawgan; from here Avro Ansons patrolled far out into the Atlantic in search of U-Boats. St Mawgan was also first landfall for the Flying Fortresses of the United States Air Force, and American airmen became a common sight in the town, bringing with them many luxuries that had not been seen for some time because of rationing.

After the war, Newquay picked up where it had left off and continued building hotels. By 1960 Narrowcliff was almost unrecognisable - most of the villas had been replaced by flat-fronted three- and four-storey structures designed to utilise space as efficiently as possible. Down in the little harbour, life continued to run with the rhythms of the seasons and the moods of the sea. Diesel had replaced sail, and the few sailing luggers left were used for pleasure rather than for earning a living, but the fishing fleet still thrived - thirty to forty boats laid their pots for lobster and crab which would end up on the table of a hotel dining room. Island Pier still stood, but the wooden tramway was demolished in the fifties; where clay wagons would once have stood, today crab pots are stacked. The pilot gigs remain, now used solely for racing, and the lifeboat sits in its boathouse, having moved to the harbour from the old station at Towan Head in 1935.

Today's lifeboat is a very different vessel from those of old, such as the 'Admiral Sir George Back' or the 'James Stevens V'. In place of oars and sails are powerful twin outboards, enabling the present boat to have completed a rescue and be back in the boathouse in less time than it took for its ancestors to be launched. But the great Atlantic swells remain, rolling relentlessly in, and by a strange quirk of fate these same swells, the ones that caused the harbour to be built in the lee of Towan Head, today help contribute to the prosperity of the town. As they hit the gradually shoaling beaches, such as Fistral and Watergate, the swells rear up into majestic lines of surf which act as a magnet for surfers.

The winter population of 20,000 reaches around 100,000 in summer, swelled by those who come to surf or just to sit around enjoying the beaches. Hotels, surf shops and night clubs flourish, and the seagulls are more likely these days to live on pasties than pilchards. The town is unrecognisable as the tiny fishing village it once was, but in one respect things have not changed so much - as it always has done, Newquay still makes its living from the sea.

TOWER ROAD 1918 68671

Tower Road takes its name from the Tower (not quite visible in this photograph) which was built in 1835 for a naval captain. Subsequent owners included the Molesworths, one of Cornwall's most famous families, and the prominent engineer Sir Richard Tangye. It is now the clubhouse of Newquay Golf Club.

CRANTOCK STREET 1918 68673

On the left is the Fire Station. The awning on the right is that of 'Little Jenk's', so called to distinguish it from 'Big Jenk's' in town. Today it is a Post Office.

BANK STREET 1912 64810A
The building just visible behind the lamppost at the far left is the Devon and Cornwall Bank, premises which are now occupied by Trueform. Hartnoll's was lit by gaslight until well into the fifties.

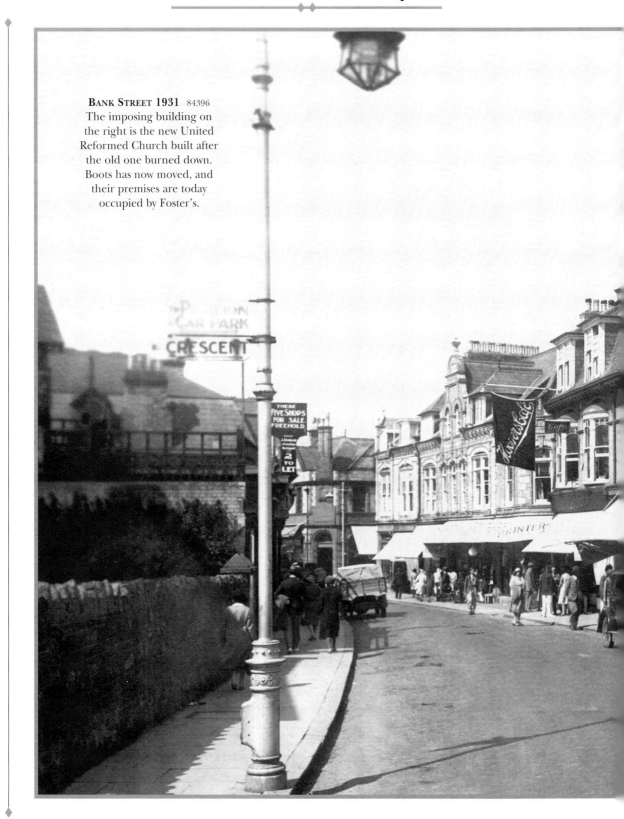

BANK STREET 1931 84396
The imposing building on the right is the new United Reformed Church built after the old one burned down. Boots has now moved, and their premises are today occupied by Foster's.

THE VICTORIA HOTEL 1900 45855

The Victoria Hotel on East Street was built at the end of the 19th century; it has a lift that runs from the hotel right down to the beach. The property to the right is now Bertie's Nightclub.

CLIFF ROAD c1960 N28198

The Great Western Hotel, which lies above the beach of the same name, was one of the first large hotels in Newquay. In 1890 a bed here would set you back the enormous sum of 5s (25p).

CLIFF TERRACE 1892
This view looks west along Cliff Road. The railway station is out of sight on the left, and the open area was the station yard, once the site of a railway turntable. The road on the right, just beyond the low wall, leads down to Great Western Beach. The long terrace of houses is now shops.

◆

NARROWCLIFF 1899
On the left is the Trenarren Hotel, and peeping out from behind it is the old Great Western Hotel building. The building on the headland on the other side of the bay is the Atlantic Hotel.

CLIFF TERRACE 1892 31172

NARROWCLIFF 1899 43169

NARROWCLIFF 1918 68672

The seats on the right look out over Tolcarne Beach. On the left, the fine houses with their characteristic dormers are still private villas - the hotel takeover has not yet begun.

NARROWCLIFF 1925 78885

This photograph was taken from the junction of Narrowcliff and Edgecumbe Avenue. Not only have the hotels taken over, but the motor car is beginning its ascendancy - note how nearly all the hotels are advertising garages. The Trenarren Hotel is today part of the Great Western Hotel, and the Runnymede is now called the Crigga Bay.

NARROWCLIFF 1925
Despite the inroads made by the car, the horse cart was still in use in the twenties. The pavements have the hard-wearing granite kerbstones so characteristic of Cornish towns.

THE TOLCARNE HOTEL 1925
That's entertainment, twenties style: dancing tonight at 8.30pm to the London Band, with Leslie Edwards, Jack Hylton's late pianist. Guests included Jack Peterson and Cornishman Len Harvey, famous heavyweight boxers of their time: after spending thirteen rounds trying to knock each other senseless in the ring, they would retire to the Tolcarne to convalesce together.

NARROWCLIFF 1925 78884

THE TOLCARNE HOTEL 1925 78886

LIFEBOAT DAY 1928 81253
Here we see the 'Admiral Sir George Beck' being
towed along Narrowcliff by the same draught horses
that were used to pull the lifeboat up the steep slip on
Towan Head. In 1935 the owner of the horses lost his
contract with the Great Western Railway and had to
sell his horses, so the lifeboat moved to the harbour.

NARROWCLIFF 1928 81261

The open area above the cliffs on the left is Barrowfields, a public open space which has at its western end a barrow (or tumulus), a Bronze Age burial site. There were once 15 barrows on Barrowfields, but all save one were razed to make way for a garage. On the far left below the clifftop is the Big Six Theatre.

NARROWCLIFF 1928 81263

This photograph was taken on Lifeboat Day, a fund-raising event which saw thousands of trippers arrive at Newquay. People dressed in their Sunday best: apparently there were even ladies in fur coats - despite the fact that the event was held on August Bank Holiday Monday.

NARROWCLIFF 1928 81262
Not only had the car established itself by
this time, but the charabanc had
appeared. Hocking's charabancs, silver
with maroon wings, took trippers on
excursions to places such as Bedruthan
Steps, the Luxulyan Valley
and Roche Rock.

NARROWCLIFF 1930 83075

On Tolcarne Beach, at the extreme left of the picture, beach huts and cafés are springing up to cater for the ever-increasing numbers of visitors. The Penolver Hotel is today part of the Beresford.

NARROWCLIFF 1930 83074

The first of the major hotel extensions on Narrowcliff has taken place: the Tolcarne Hotel is now four storeys high, and almost unrecognisable, save for the two bay windows of the original frontage which have been preserved.

NARROWCLIFF C1960 N28192
Narrowcliff now looks very different from how it did in the twenties. Many of the hotels have followed the Tolcarne's lead and erected imposing frontages. Only the Cliffdene, on the left, preserves the look of the original villas.

EDGECUMBE AVENUE 1918 68677
Edgecumbe Avenue is named after local landowner Robert Edgecumbe, and leads inland from Narrowcliff towards Trenance. The building on the right is now Trevanion Flats, and the middle part of the other side of the road is today occupied by the Elliot Garth Hotel.

EDGECUMBE AVENUE 1907 59339

EDGECUMBE AVENUE 1907
Is the man in the straw boater thinking of buying? The house has only recently been completed, for the sign in the garden bears the names of the tradesmen involved: George Clark, Builder; George Card, Architect; H Checwidden, Decorator and J Penberthy, Plumber.

TRENANCE GARDENS c1960
Trenance Gardens and Lake were created in 1932 by unemployed men, who were given a hot meal and tobacco in payment. In the background is the current Trenance Viaduct, completed in 1938 and bringing the branch line from Par.

TRENANCE GARDENS c1960 N28181

THE HOSPITAL 1931

The hospital on St Thomas' Road was opened by the Duke of Kent on one of his frequent visits to Newquay. Today it occupies the same site, but it is much altered and vastly extended.

◆

TREWERRY MILL 1907

Trewerry Mill lies three miles inland on a tributary of the Gannel not far from Trerice Manor, and now serves cream teas.

THE HOSPITAL 1931 84401

TREWERRY MILL 1907 59351

TRENANCE VIADUCT 1907 59338
Trenance Viaduct was first constructed in 1849
to bring china clay to Newquay Harbour. It was
originally a precarious-looking structure known as the
'Trenance Spider'; the arrival of the railway meant
that it had to be replaced with this more robust
structure in 1874.

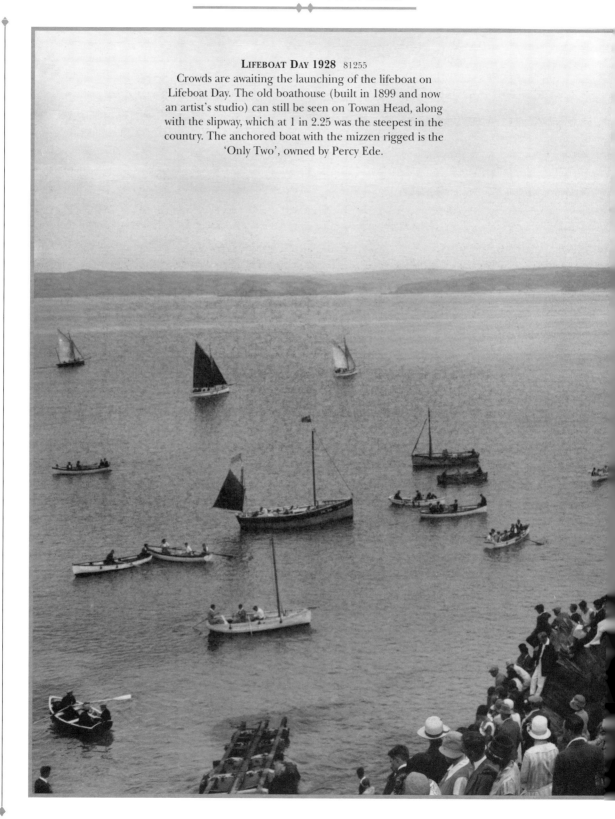

LIFEBOAT DAY 1928 81255
Crowds are awaiting the launching of the lifeboat on
Lifeboat Day. The old boathouse (built in 1899 and now
an artist's studio) can still be seen on Towan Head, along
with the slipway, which at 1 in 2.25 was the steepest in the
country. The anchored boat with the mizzen rigged is the
'Only Two', owned by Percy Ede.

LAUNCHING THE LIFEBOAT 1928 81254

The lifeboat being launched here on Lifeboat Day is the 'Admiral Sir George Back', which was stationed at Newquay from 1921-35. It had ten oars and sails, and was last launched in 1934. The boys visible at the sides of the boat would jump off after the launch and collect money from the crowds in their red RNLI hats.

TOWAN HEAD 1892 31170

The building on the headland is a fish cellar. The cove in the foreground is where the Newquay lifeboat, the 'James Steven V', was lost in 1917.

THE HEADLAND HOTEL 1900
When the Headland Hotel was built, the Hotel company enclosed an area of common land where fishermen had traditionally laid out their nets to dry. The fishermen demonstrated 'riotously' and won the concession of having the headland leased to the town council in return for not disrupting the building of the hotel.

◆

THE HEADLAND HOTEL AND FISTRAL BAY 1901
The imposing edifice of the Headland Hotel was completed in 1900. It was designed by the celebrated Cornish architect Sylvanus Trevail, who was also chairman of the hotel company. The windows above the conservatory are those of the Royal Suite. During World War Two the hotel was used as an amputating hospital.

THE HEADLAND HOTEL 1900 45860

THE HEADLAND HOTEL AND FISTRAL BAY 1901 47744

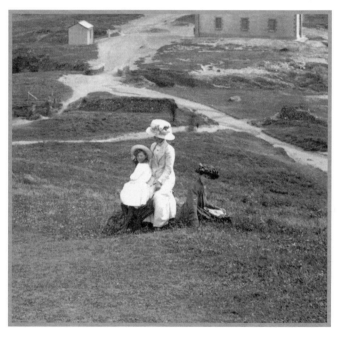

**THE ATLANTIC
AND HEADLAND HOTELS 1912** 64804
The Atlantic Hotel (left, on the
headland) was the first large hotel to be
built in Newquay. Built between 1890
and 1892, its architect was also Sylvanus
Trevail. The old Lifeboat House (right,
with three windows) was built back from
the shore so as not to spoil the view from
the Headland Hotel.

THE BEACON 1894 33525

This quaint little building was once used by H M Coastguard. It is now under the war memorial, which was unveiled by The Prince of Wales in 1921. In the background is the Atlantic Hotel.

THE HUER'S HUT 1907 59333

The endearingly ugly Huer's Hut, standing on King Edward Crescent, is a reminder of Newquay's great days as a fishing port. Its exact age is unknown, but it could date from as early as the 14th century; it was used as a lookout for fish shoals.

THE HUER'S HUT 1914 66673A

Open on the seaward side, and with no glazing in the windows, the Huer's Hut must have been a draughty place; it probably needed its enormous chimney merely to keep the watchers warm. It was one of several strategic points from which men with large flags directed the seine boats in the difficult process of ringing the pilchard shoals.

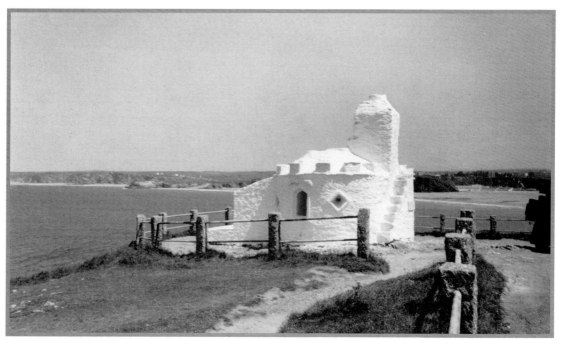

THE HUER'S HUT 1960 N28285

The Huer's Hut was restored in 1835 by a man named Vivian who, appropriately, was paid in fish for his endeavours. Newquay Town Council took over the lease of the building for a peppercorn rent in 1906.

FROM THE FISH CELLARS 1887 20244
Over a hundred feet high, the rampart
of Towan Head shelters the harbour
from the brunt of the fierce westerlies
that sweep in from the Atlantic. On the
point (right) is Fly Fish Cellars; the long
low building in the centre is
Active Fish Cellars.

THE HARBOUR 1894 33521
The wooden trestle pier (known locally as the Jetty)
connects South Pier to Island Pier, which was built in
1872 to increase the capacity of the harbour. The
prominent house on the hill above the masts of the
schooner was the residence of the
Chief Constable of Cornwall.

THE HARBOUR 1894 33518

Hidden at the end of the pier (centre) is the entrance to the tunnel that comes through the cliffs to allow railway wagons to bring cargoes to ships in the harbour. The tunnel emerged where Somerfield now stands on Fore Street.

THE HARBOUR 1894 33522

This photograph was taken from Eli Clemen's boatyard. The squat building on the cliff (left) was a grain store: from it grain ran down chutes to be loaded into vessels moored by the cliff just by the white boat.

FROM THE HARBOUR c1900

At the end of South Pier are empty wagons, and alongside the ship full ones, probably awaiting high tide to make loading possible. At the top of the beach on the right are the old fish cellars, now far less busy since the collapse of the pilchard stocks around 1870.

THE HARBOUR 1907

Compare this picture with photograph No N28502 to see just how fast Newquay was growing - almost all the gaps in the skyline have been filled with houses and hotels. In 1850, Newquay was still a small fishing village, but by 1907 the population was approaching 4,000.

FROM THE HARBOUR c1900 N28502

THE HARBOUR 1907 59327

THE HARBOUR 1907 59328
Moored at bottom right are two traditional luggers, possibly built at St Ives, and the mainstay of the fishing fleet. The 'Ethel' (far right), by comparison, was a pleasure craft.

ENTRANCE TO THE HARBOUR 1921 70854
Like many Cornish harbours, that at Newquay has a very narrow entrance to protect vessels in harbour during heavy weather. The round structure on the right used to have an oil-fired red light which indicated the port entrance to the harbour. Today the job is done by electricity.

THE HARBOUR 1925 78866

The trestle pier still stands, but the harbour appears almost lifeless when compared with the bustle of 1894. The white boat in the centre foreground is a fishing gig, built without a centre thwart to allow nets to be carried.

THE RED LION HOTEL 1888 21185

Overlooking the harbour from North Quay Hill, the Red Lion Hotel is one of the oldest in the town, built around 130 years ago. Originally called Prout's Hotel, it started life as a coaching inn.

THE HARBOUR 1930

This photograph demonstrates just how sheltered Newquay harbour is, tucked into the lee of Towan head. While the storm rages around the rocks and beaches of Newquay Bay opposite, the boats in the harbour bob gently. The white boat second from right is the 'Sunny South', which later became an exhibit at Exeter Maritime Museum.

THE HARBOUR c1960

The last traces of industrial Cornwall have gone. The trestle pier was demolished in 1950, leaving Island Pier as an island, and all trace of the railway lines has vanished. The building with the white windows on the harbourside (left) is the mission and reading room, standing roughly where the lifeboat station is now.

THE HARBOUR 1930 83061

THE HARBOUR c1960 N28173

The Harbour from the Sands c1960 N28203

The harbour is now a place of pleasure rather than commerce. Tourists (including one woman who may or may not have been to Mexico) enjoy the beach, and most of the boats are diesel powered. The boat moored at Island Pier belonged to Pip Staffieri, maker of the best ice creams in Cornwall.

The Harbour c1960 N28245

Drawn up on the beach at centre is a small fleet of pilot gigs, light and manoeuvrable six-oared boats about 30 feet long and just under five feet wide. They were used by ship-handling companies up to the 19th century to take pilots out to incoming boats.

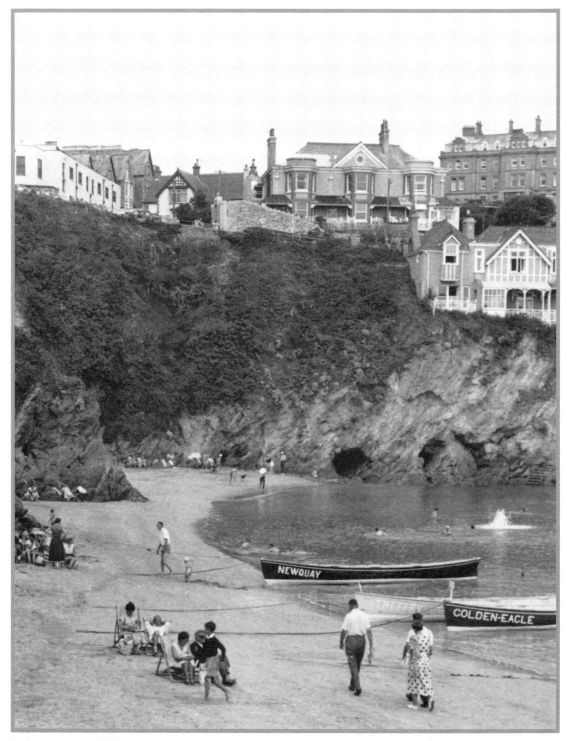

THE HARBOUR c1960 N28264

For the crews of the pilot gigs, speed was of the essence to ensure that their pilot was the one that got the pillage fee, and so there arose a great rivalry between crews: this led eventually to the sport of pilot gig racing.

THE HARBOUR c1960

Gigs travel from port to port to take part in regattas; 'Shah' comes from St Agnes and 'Golden Eagle' and 'Bonnet' from St Mary's in the Isles of Scilly, spiritual home of gig racing. 'Ternary' (Newquay) is one of the fastest gigs afloat, and it is on her lines that most modern gigs are built. The oldest gig is the 'Newquay', built in 1812 and still

◆

THE HARBOUR c1960

Changing modes of transport: a fine selection of classic cars is parked on South Pier where the railway tracks once ran. They include a Morris Minor van, a Ford Consul, an Austin A30 and a Humber Snipe. The little white building is the Harbourmaster's Office.

THE HARBOUR c1960   N28265

THE HARBOUR c1960   N28268

THE SANDS 1901 47733
In the year of Queen Victoria's death, Victorian values
obviously still applied: drawn up on the beach just
above the water are twenty or so bathing machines,
designed to preserve the dignity of women bathers
and not outrage public decency.

TOWAN BEACH 1921 70851

The long low roof on the left is Speculation Fish Cellar. In the centre is the domed roof of the Pavilion Cinema (opened by George Robey), and the long terrace just below the skyline on the right is the coastguard cottages.

TOWAN BEACH LOOKING EAST 1921 70848

The prominent church tower on the skyline is that of the Wesleyan Methodist church, built in 1904, which still stands on East Street. The architects originally planned for it to have a spire, but this was never built. The field above Towan Beach was still grazed by bullocks from Killacourt Farm.

TOWAN BEACH 1933 85999

It is a mere thirty years after photograph No 47733, and the beach scene is quite different. There are many more people, probably from all classes, and the bathing machines have been consigned to history. Some of the swimming costumes on display, while modest by today's standards, would have caused quite a stir in Victorian

FEEDING THE GULLS c1960 N28208

Don't try this today! Herring gulls, one of our most adaptable species, are noisy, opportunistic scavengers with a taste for pasties and fish and chips - and tourist's fingers. It is interesting to speculate whether Alfred Hitchcock ever visited Newquay.

THE SANDS AND THE ISLAND 1907 59320
Before the building of the famous suspension bridge in 1900, the Island was known as Jago's Island and used for keeping chickens. There was a café on the summit before the house was built in 1910.

THE ISLAND AND THE SUSPENSION BRIDGE c1960 N28165
The private house atop the Island has had various owners, including the Lodge family. Sir Oliver Joseph Lodge invented the spark plug; he numbered among his friends Sir Arthur Conan Doyle, who is said to have stayed several times on the Island.

DANCING ON THE BEACH 1912 64790A
Newquay Town Band wear white hats
and play exclusively brass instruments.
The black hats and clarinet (left)
indicate that this may well be the
German band, which visited regularly at
one time. The big hotel on the clifftop is
the Edgecumbe, which later
burned down.

ON THE SANDS 1912 64802
Here we see a beach party composed entirely of the
fairer sex - with the exception of the rather lost-
looking little boy standing between the two girls at the
back. Perhaps this was an outing from a girls' school
or a convent. In the background is the
Great Western Hotel

LUSTY GLAZE BEACH c1960 N28237

This picture shows all the traditional paraphernalia of a day out on the beach: deck chairs, rubber rings, surf boards and chalets. Lusty Glaze is the last of Newquay's beaches before the little inlet of Porth.

CRIGGA ROCKS 1925 78882

The enduring appeal of the beach: change the costumes, and the scene could be today. In the background, the woman in the pale dress appears to be doing the one-footed dance familiar to all who have ever tried to change while simultaneously preserving modesty and avoiding the perils of sand in the underwear.

PORTH 1925 78901

Along with the Gannel, Porth was one of the original ports of Newquay, and between 1818 and 1880 was used for shipbuilding. The long low building in the centre is Steven's yard, used for storing coal and other cargoes landed on the beach.

PORTH BRIDGE 1912 64815

Porth Bridge joins Porth Island or Trevelgue Head to the mainland. The earliest bridge was over 2,000 years ago, when Trevelgue Head was an Iron Age fort similar to many of the cliff castles built on Cornish headlands. Beyond the bridge, just round the corner, was the 'Banqueting Hall', a vast sea-cave which was often used for functions. If music was called for, a piano would be carried through the gully past where the little boy is standing!

THE WATERGATE HOTEL 1900 45858

The Watergate Hotel was built around the turn of the century in the false hope that the new railway was coming to nearby St Columb Major. It was designed by John Ennor, who also designed Newquay's sewage system. Famous guests included Baron von Richtofen. It continued in use as a hotel until World War Two, when it was requisitioned for use as an officers' mess.

WATERGATE BAY 1918 68664

After World War Two, the hotel became married quarters; then it stood empty until 1967, when it was turned into holiday flats. Over the winter of 1970-71 it was converted back to a hotel by Mr and Mrs Ashworth.

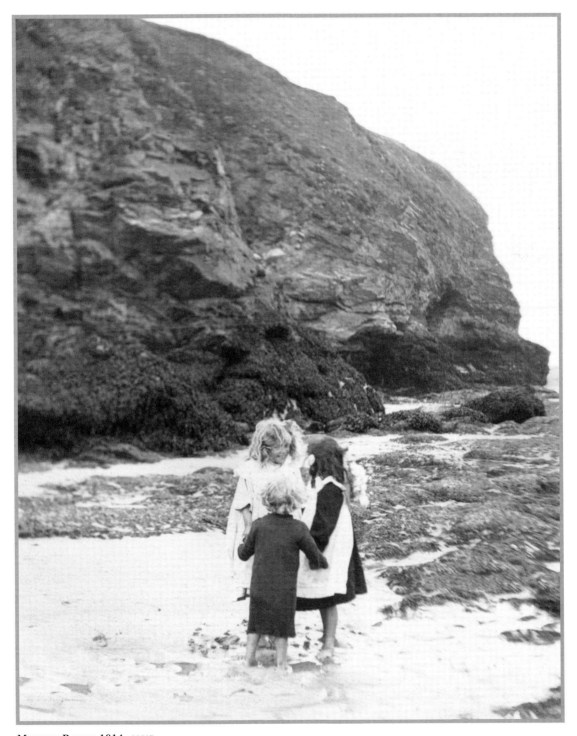

MAWGAN PORTH 1914 66687
Mawgan Porth lies three miles north of Newquay at the mouth of the pretty Vale of Mawgan, which runs inland to St Columb Major. On the hills above the vale is RAF St Mawgan, home of the search and reconnaissance Nimrods which patrol far out into the Atlantic.

CRANTOCK, FROM EAST PENTIRE 1887 20285

Crantock lies to the south-east of Newquay, opposite Pentire and on the south side of the Gannel (seen, at low tide, in the foreground). To reach Crantock from Pentire is a matter of a few minutes by ferry or on foot at the lowest of tides; the same journey by car round the head of the estuary is nearly five miles.

CRANTOCK, THE CHURCH 1899 43795

Crantock takes its name from St Garantoc, an Irish missionary who in AD 460 founded an oratory on the site. The present church is 16th-century; in this picture it is midway through restoration, having been neglected and fallen into decay in the 19th century.

CRANTOCK, THE VILLAGE 1912 64819
George Metford Parsons, who was Vicar from 1894 to 1924, was the inspiration for the rebuilding of the church, which was completed in 1902. A final touch was the addition of a clock, missing in photograph No 43795.

CRANTOCK, THE VILLAGE 1912 64820

The thatched white building on the left is now a private house. It was once the Ship Inn, which closed down during the Temperance movement that swept Cornwall in the 1830s as a response to the excessive drinking brought about by the smuggling of brandy.

CRANTOCK, THE POST OFFICE 1918 68678

The Post Office is now also the village shop, and extends into the rooms hidden by the bush. The clump of trees at the junction in the background surround what is now Crantock Round Garden, originally built as a pound to enclose stray animals from nearby commons.

CRANTOCK, THE VILLAGE 1935 86710
The little building on the left is Crantock Memorial Hall, built after the First World War and now also commemorating the dead of World War Two. Today it is used for community events.

CRANTOCK, BEACH ROAD c1960 C181008
The centre of Crantock today is little changed, save for the telegraph poles and metalled roads. The curious conical structure in the centre was once the village well.

CRANTOCK, WEST PENTIRE 1936 87614

On the right is Crantock Beach at the mouth of The Gannel; beyond is Pentire Point East, which has Bronze Age burial mounds, or tumuli. The rocky island in the centre is The Goose. The large building is the West Pentire Hotel.

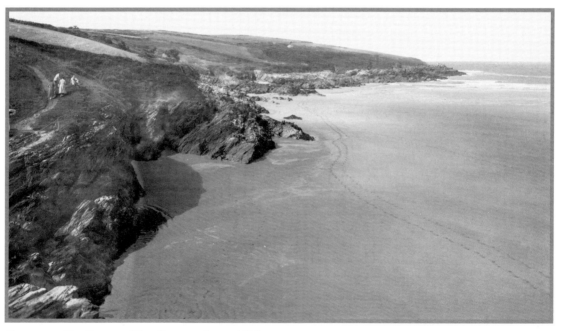

CRANTOCK, THE BAY AND WEST PENTIRE SANDS 1936 87615

Hidden round the corner of the headland is Pentire Point West, now owned by the National Trust, and beyond that is the charming little cove of Porth Joke. The footsteps in the sand might be heading for Vugga Cove, hidden on the left and once the haunt of smugglers.

CRANTOCK,
East Pentire and Towan Heads 1936
Pentire Point East is the nearest
headland, and poking out from behind
it is Towan Head. The shadowy coastline
in the background runs north north
west for twelve miles to Trevose Head,
just visible on the left of the picture.

FERN PIT ON THE GANNEL 1901
On the left is a houseboat, long since
gone, and to its right the little quay was
the landing place for the ferry. Boats
could be hired here for an afternoon
messing about on the Gannel.

CRANTOCK, EAST PENTIRE AND TOWAN HEADS 1936 87617

FERN PIT ON THE GANNEL 1901 47747

FERN PIT AND WEST PENTIRE 1904 52303

Fern Pit, owned by successive generations of Northeys, was a popular tea room. In 1938 a huge quantity of pit props from a wreck was washed up on Crantock Beach. The locals put them to good use.

PENTIRE, THE GANNEL c1955 P359006

In the 18th century Welsh coal was landed on the Gannel, at Penpol (hidden at centre right) and at Trevemper, at the head of the estuary in the far distance. Today the estuary is choked with sand and far too shallow for large

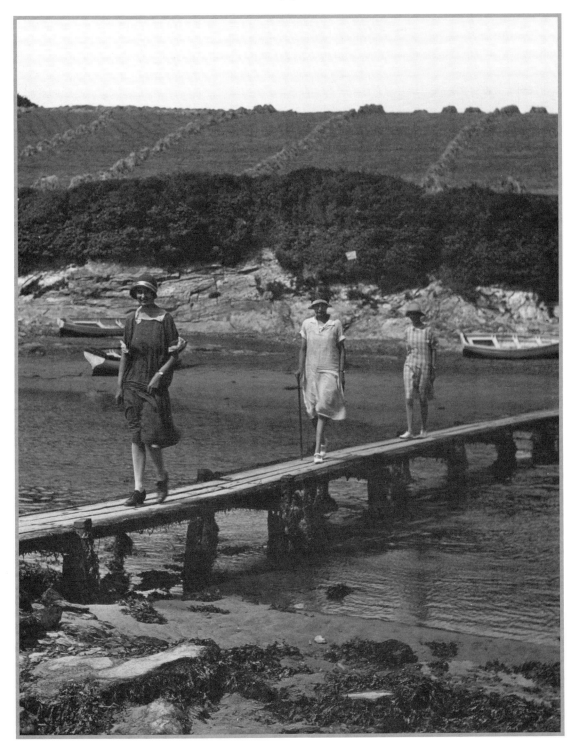

CROSSING THE GANNEL 1925 78898
In the field on the hill behind, stooks of corn from Trethelan Farm are stacked to dry. The hill is now built up, but the little bridge survives, negotiable only at low tide.

THE RIVER GANNEL 1928 81295
The River Gannel (Cornish for 'channel' or 'crooked estuary') rises inland near the chapel at Fraddon and flows ten miles to reach its estuary. Here at the Gannel Regatta the race in progress is for outboard motor boats, and is being led by Edward Jenkin in 'Maquarie'.

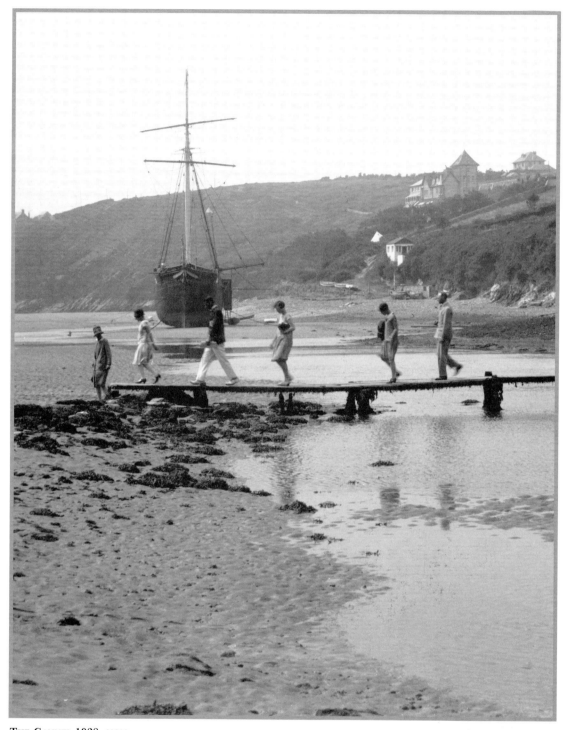

THE GANNEL 1928 81300

This pictures harks back to more prosperous time for The Gannel. In the mid 19th century it was an important boat building area, with sailing schooners being built on the foreshore. The schooner here is the 'Ada', which later became a museum on Penpol Creek.

THE GANNEL 1928

Here we see the crossing from the south side of the Gannel to Newquay by ferry. Ferries such as this are common on Cornish estuaries, and are often summoned by shouting or whistling. Here Dick Northey, who owned Fern Pit, is bringing the ferry in on Crantock Beach.

PENTIRE
Fistral Bay c1955

Facing west, directly into the Atlantic swells, and with a gently sloping beach, Fistral Bay has some of the best surf in the country; it is regularly the venue for competitions, including, on occasion, the World Championships. The large building on the other side of the bay is the Headland Hotel.

THE GANNEL 1928 81302

PENTIRE, FISTRAL BAY c1955 P359009

FISTRAL BAY c1960
This photograph was taken from the north end of Fistral Beach, just where the road leads to the corner of the beach in photograph No P359009. Pentire Point East is the obvious headland, with The Goose just to the right. The large building on the skyline is the Pentire Hotel.

PENTIRE 1918
This view looks back inland to another age: there are still wide open spaces between the houses, the road is not made up, and there are no street lights or overhead cables.

FISTRAL BAY c1960 N28286

PENTIRE 1918 68688

PENTIRE 1918 68646

On the far left skyline are the exposed houses of Atlantic Road. The house with the arched doorway just right of centre was built by R J Clemens and is now flats.

PENTIRE, THE BAY HOTEL 1928 81273

In the ten years after photograph No 68646 the area is considerably more built up; the house in the centre of the picture is now surrounded, and the Bay Hotel (also built by R J Clemens) has doubled in size.

THE GOLF COURSE 1907 59337
The long low building is the Clubhouse, and behind it
is the Tower. At one time, before Sunday golf, the golf
course was a popular spot for Sunday picnics.

PENTIRE, THE COAST FROM THE GOLF LINKS c1955 P359003
Newquay Golf Links was laid out in the 1890s and enjoys a fine view over Fistral Bay and out towards Pentire Point East. Prince Edward (later Edward VIII and then Duke of Windsor) played golf here.

THE GOLF LINKS 1925 78891
This picture shows just why Fistral Beach is such a Mecca for surfers - long lines of clean, evenly breaking surf. But in 1925 there appears not to be a surfer in sight - the sport had not yet arrived from California.

ATLANTIC ROAD 1918

The fine terrace of Atlantic Road runs parallel to Higher Tower Road and has magnificent views out over Fistral Beach. The downside is the wind - local lore has it that there were always one or two houses empty here because of the exposed position! At the far end of the road is the old cemetery.

PENTIRE
View from the Post Office c1955

How quiet the street seems! No road markings, no double yellow lines and no cars. The grassy patch beyond the telephone box was the national Children's Home playground, and the hotel on the far right was the St Rumon, now the esplanade.

ATLANTIC ROAD 1918   68676

PENTIRE, VIEW FROM THE POST OFFICE c1955   P359004

THE FISTRAL BAY HOTEL 1931 84399
The Fistral Bay Hotel was built at around the turn of the century. The bus going down the hill belongs to Western National - the same company that runs the bus service today.

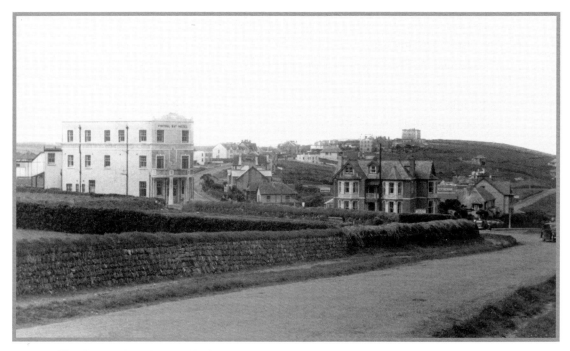

PENTIRE, THE FISTRAL BAY HOTEL c1955 P359010
Here we see another view of the Fistral Bay Hotel, but now with three storeys rather than two. The extra storey was added sometime before World War Two.

Index

Frith Book Co Titles

Frith Book Company publish over a 100 new titles each year. For latest catalogue please contact Frith Book Co.

Town Books 96pp, 100 photos. County and Themed Books 128pp, 150 photos
(unless specified) All titles hardback laminated case and jacket
except those indicated pb (paperback)

Around Barnstaple	1-85937-084-5	£12.99
Around Blackpool	1-85937-049-7	£12.99
Around Bognor Regis	1-85937-055-1	£12.99
Around Bristol	1-85937-050-0	£12.99
Around Cambridge	1-85937-092-6	£12.99
Cheshire	1-85937-045-4	£14.99
Around Chester	1-85937-090-X	£12.99
Around Chesterfield	1-85937-071-3	£12.99
Around Chichester	1-85937-089-6	£12.99
Cornwall	1-85937-054-3	£14.99
Cotswolds	1-85937-099-3	£14.99
Around Derby	1-85937-046-2	£12.99
Devon	1-85937-052-7	£14.99
Dorset	1-85937-075-6	£14.99
Dorset Coast	1-85937-062-4	£14.99
Around Dublin	1-85937-058-6	£12.99
East Anglia	1-85937-059-4	£14.99
Around Eastbourne	1-85937-061-6	£12.99
English Castles	1-85937-078-0	£14.99
Around Falmouth	1-85937-066-7	£12.99
Hampshire	1-85937-064-0	£14.99
Isle of Man	1-85937-065-9	£14.99
Around Maidstone	1-85937-056-X	£12.99
North Yorkshire	1-85937-048-9	£14.99
Around Nottingham	1-85937-060-8	£12.99
Around Penzance	1-85937-069-1	£12.99
Around Reading	1-85937-087-X	£12.99
Around St Ives	1-85937-068-3	£12.99
Around Salisbury	1-85937-091-8	£12.99
Around Scarborough	1-85937-104-3	£12.99
Scottish Castles	1-85937-077-2	£14.99
Around Sevenoaks and Tonbridge	1-85937-057-8	£12.99

Sheffield and S Yorkshire	1-85937-070-5	£14.99
Shropshire	1-85937-083-7	£14.99
Staffordshire	1-85937-047-0 (96pp)	£12.99
Suffolk	1-85937-074-8	£14.99
Surrey	1-85937-081-0	£14.99
Around Torbay	1-85937-063-2	£12.99
Wiltshire	1-85937-053-5	£14.99
Around Bakewell	1-85937-113-2	£12.99
Around Bournemouth	1-85937-067-5	£12.99
Cambridgeshire	1-85937-086-1	£14.99
Essex	1-85937-082-9	£14.99
Around Great Yarmouth	1-85937-085-3	£12.99
Hertfordshire	1-85937-079-9	£14.99
Isle of Wight	1-85937-114-0	£14.99
Around Lincoln	1-85937-111-6	£12.99
Oxfordshire	1-85937-076-4	£14.99
Around Shrewsbury	1-85937-110-8	£12.99
South Devon Coast	1-85937-107-8	£14.99
Around Stratford upon Avon	1-85937-098-5	£12.99
West Midlands	1-85937-109-4	£14.99

British Life A Century Ago
246 x 189mm
144pp, hardback.
Black and white
Lavishly illustrated with photos
from the turn of the century,
and with extensive commentary.
It offers a unique insight into
the social history and heritage
of bygone Britain.

1-85937-103-5 £17.99

Available from your local bookshop or from the publisher

Frith Book Co Titles Available in 2000

Around Bath	1-85937-097-7	£12.99	Mar
County Durham	1-85937-123-x	£14.99	Mar
Cumbria	1-85937-101-9	£14.99	Mar
Down the Thames	1-85937-121-3	£14.99	Mar
Around Exeter	1-85937-126-4	£12.99	Mar
Greater Manchester	1-85937-108-6	£14.99	Mar
Around Guildford	1-85937-117-5	£12.99	Mar
Around Harrogate	1-85937-112-4	£12.99	Mar
Around Leicester	1-85937-073-x	£12.99	Mar
Around Liverpool	1-85937-051-9	£12.99	Mar
Around Newark	1-85937-105-1	£12.99	Mar
Northumberland and Tyne & Wear			
	1-85937-072-1	£14.99	Mar
Around Oxford	1-85937-096-9	£12.99	Mar
Around Plymouth	1-85937-119-1	£12.99	Mar
Around Southport	1-85937-106-x	£12.99	Mar
Welsh Castles	1-85937-120-5	£14.99	Mar
Around Belfast	1-85937-094-2	£12.99	Apr
Canals and Waterways	1-85937-129-9	£17.99	Apr
Down the Severn	1-85937-118-3	£14.99	Apr
East Sussex	1-85937-130-2	£14.99	Apr
Exmoor	1-85937-132-9	£14.99	Apr
Gloucestershire	1-85937-102-7	£14.99	Apr
Around Horsham	1-85937-127-2	£12.99	Apr
Around Ipswich	1-85937-133-7	£12.99	Apr
Ireland (pb)	1-85937-181-7	£9.99	Apr
Kent Living Memories	1-85937-125-6	£14.99	Apr
London (pb)	1-85937-183-3	£9.99	Apr
New Forest	1-85937-128-0	£14.99	Apr
Scotland (pb)	1-85937-182-5	£9.99	Apr
Around Southampton	1-85937-088-8	£12.99	Apr
Stone Circles & Ancient Monuments			
	1-85937-143-4	£17.99	Apr
Sussex (pb)	1-85937-184-1	£9.99	Apr
Colchester (pb)	1-85937-188-4	£8.99	May
County Maps of Britain			
	1-85937-156-6 (192pp)	£19.99	May
Leicestershire (pb)	1-85937-185-x	£9.99	May

Lincolnshire	1-85937-135-3	£14.99	May
Around Newquay	1-85937-140-x	£12.99	May
Nottinghamshire (pb)	1-85937-187-6	£9.99	May
Redhill to Reigate	1-85937-137-x	£12.99	May
Victorian & Edwardian Yorkshire			
	1-85937-154-x	£14.99	May
Around Winchester	1-85937-139-6	£12.99	May
Yorkshire (pb)	1-85937-186-8	£9.99	May
Berkshire (pb)	1-85937-191-4	£9.99	Jun
Brighton (pb)	1-85937-192-2	£8.99	Jun
Dartmoor	1-85937-145-0	£14.99	Jun
East London	1-85937-080-2	£14.99	Jun
Glasgow (pb)	1-85937-190-6	£8.99	Jun
Kent (pb)	1-85937-189-2	£9.99	Jun
Victorian & Edwardian Kent			
	1-85937-149-3	£14.99	Jun
North Devon Coast	1-85937-146-9	£14.99	Jun
Peak District	1-85937-100-0	£14.99	Jun
Around Truro	1-85937-147-7	£12.99	Jun
Victorian & Edwardian Maritime Album			
	1-85937-144-2	£17.99	Jun
West Sussex	1-85937-148-5	£14.99	Jun
Churches of Berkshire	1-85937-170-1	£17.99	Jul
Churches of Dorset	1-85937-172-8	£17.99	Jul
Churches of Hampshire	1-85937-207-4	£17.99	Jul
Churches of Wiltshire	1-85937-171-x	£17.99	Jul
Derbyshire (pb)	1-85937-196-5	£9.99	Jul
Edinburgh (pb)	1-85937-193-0	£8.99	Jul
Herefordshire	1-85937-174-4	£14.99	Jul
Norwich (pb)	1-85937-194-9	£8.99	Jul
Ports and Harbours	1-85937-208-2	£17.99	Jul
Somerset and Avon	1-85937-153-1	£14.99	Jul
South Devon Living Memories			
	1-85937-168-x	£14.99	Jul
Warwickshire (pb)	1-85937-203-1	£9.99	Jul
Worcestershire	1-85937-152-3	£14.99	Jul
Yorkshire Living Memories			
	1-85937-166-3	£14.99	Jul

FRITH PRODUCTS & SERVICES

Francis Frith would doubtless be pleased to know that the pioneering publishing venture he started in 1860 still continues today. More than a hundred and thirty years later, The Francis Frith Collection continues in the same innovative tradition and is now one of the foremost publishers of vintage photographs in the world. Some of the current activities include:

Interior Decoration

Today Frith's photographs can be seen framed and as giant wall murals in thousands of pubs, restaurants, hotels, banks, retail stores and other public buildings throughout the country. In every case they enhance the unique local atmosphere of the places they depict and provide reminders of gentler days in an increasingly busy and frenetic world.

Product Promotions

Frith products have been used by many major companies to promote the sales of their own products or to reinforce their own history and heritage. Brands include Hovis bread, Courage beers, Scots Porage Oats, Colman's mustard, Cadbury's foods, Mellow Birds coffee, Dunhill pipe tobacco, Guinness, and Bulmer's Cider.

Genealogy and Family History

As the interest in family history and roots grows world-wide, more and more people are turning to Frith's photographs of Great Britain for images of the towns, villages and streets where their ancestors lived; and, of course, photographs of the churches and chapels where their ancestors were christened, married and buried are an essential part of every genealogy tree and family album.

A series of easy-to-use CD Roms is planned for publication, and an increasing number of Frith photographs will be able to be viewed on specialist genealogy sites. A growing range of Frith books will be available on CD.

The Internet

Already thousands of Frith photographs can be viewed and purchased on the internet. By the end of the year 2000 some 60,000 Frith photographs will be available on the internet. The number of sites is constantly expanding, each focussing on different products and services from the Collection.

Some of the sites are listed below.

www.townpages.co.uk
www.icollector.com
www.barclaysquare.co.uk
www.cornwall-online.co.uk

For background information on the Collection look at the three following sites:

www.francisfrith.com
www.francisfrith.co.uk
www.frithbook.co.uk

Frith Products

All Frith photographs are available Framed or just as Mounted Prints, and can be ordered from the address below. From time to time other products - Address Books, Calendars, Table Mats, etc - are available.

For further information:
if you would like further information on any of the above aspects of the Frith business please contact us at the address below:
The Francis Frith Collection,
Frith's Barn, Teffont, Salisbury, Wiltshire,
England SP3 5QP.
Tel: +44 (0)1722 716 376 Fax: +44 (0)1722 716 881 Email: uksales@francisfrith.com

To receive your FREE Mounted Print

Mounted Print
Overall size 14 x 11 inches

Cut out this Voucher and return it with your remittance for £1.50 to cover postage and handling. Choose any photograph included in this book. Your SEPIA print will be A4 in size, and mounted in a cream mount with burgundy rule lines, overall size 14 x 11 inches.

Order additional Mounted Prints at HALF PRICE (only £7.49 each*)

If there are further pictures you would like to order, possibly as gifts for friends and family, acquire them at half price (no additional postage and handling required).

Have your Mounted Prints framed*

For an additional £14.95 per print you can have your chosen Mounted Print framed in an elegant polished wood and gilt moulding, overall size 16 x 13 inches (no additional postage and handling required).

---

* IMPORTANT!
These special prices are only available if ordered using the original voucher on this page (no copies permitted) and at the same time as your free Mounted Print, for delivery to the same address

---

Frith Collectors' Guild

From time to time we publish a magazine of news and stories about Frith photographs and further special offers of Frith products. If you would like 12 months FREE membership, please return this form.

Send completed forms to:
**The Francis Frith Collection,
Frith's Barn, Teffont, Salisbury,
Wiltshire SP3 5QP**

---

 for FREE and Reduced Price Frith Prints

Picture no.	Page number	Qty	Mounted @ £7.49	Framed + £14.95	Total Cost
		1	**Free of charge***	£	£
			£7.49	£	£
			£7.49	£	£
			£7.49	£	£
			£7.49	£	£
			£7.49	£	£
			* Post & handling		£1.50
Book Title			**Total Order Cost**		£

Please do not photocopy this voucher. Only the original is valid, so please cut it out and return it to us.

I enclose a cheque / postal order for £ . . . . made payable to 'The Francis Frith Collection'
OR please debit my Mastercard / Visa / Switch / Amex card

Number . . . .

Expires . . . . Signature . . . .

Name Mr/Mrs/Ms . . . .

Address . . . .

. . . .

. . . .

. . . . Postcode . . . .

Daytime Tel No . . . .   Valid to 31/12/01

The Francis Frith Collectors' Guild

Please enrol me as a member for 12 months free of charge.

Name Mr/Mrs/Ms . . . .

Address . . . .

. . . .

. . . .

. . . . Postcode . . . .